Stars Light: Seventh Volume

Lights of the Dead

Abol Danesh

 www.trafford.com

North America & international
toll-free: 1 888 232 4444 (USA & Canada)
fax: 812 355 4082

DEDICATION

This book is dedicated to my daughters
Shabnam and Sheida.

Acknowledgements

I seize this opportunity to thank the entire Trafford Publishing Team for their professional assistance and friendly collegiality toward publication of the Seventh and the Eighth volumes of Stars Light. In particular, my heartfelt appreciation goes to May Brown, Michelle Chandler, Heidi Morgan, Jill Serinas and Evan Villadores who helped me in each step of the way to get these two volumes off the ground all the way to the finishing line of publication production to the delight of our esteemed readers and critics.

My special thanks also goes to my wife, Sholeh, for always being supportive of my work and my artistic endeavors. Most of my artistry work most of the time have appeared so esoteric, eccentric, outlandish, and estrange to her, including my daughters as well, who have come together in a triad to name my work in a friendly satire-- The Hassan Land

The number of people who have inspired my work are endless and I wish them all happiness, joy, and above all asking them for their continuous friendship.

It goes without saying that if there are errors and shortcomings they are all mine and I take full responsibility, and I will be working hard to improve them in the next edition.

Contents

Acknowledgment..vii
Introduction xiii

Turmoil Running Down Lava 1
ANCINET 2
Food and Drink: Camelot Revisiting the Infinity 3
Imagining Colors 4
In Praise of Laziness 5
Flow of Life 6
Naked Earth, Naked Sky, Thunderbolts......................7
Lone Bird Star 8
Bolts...9
Fresh Start 10
On a Grand Scale and on Large Scheme of Things....12
XXX..13
In Search of Privacy 14
Social Oxygen 15
Ocean Water Sand Clock...16
Without Tomb Stone 18
The Country 19
"ONE" 22
Cook the Messiah 23
Original Sin Revisited..24
Repetition: To Have a Good Time.............................25
Talk Obesity 26
Distinct Possibilities in Number 27
I Am in Pain...28

The Moment, the Momentum, and the Momentous .29
Drink water without kissing it 30
My Claim: MC 31
It Is All About the Lips! The Supreme! 32
Trojan War 33
Anonymous...34
Heart of Stones...35
Silver and Gold: Christmas is a good time of the
year 36
Afar..37
Palm 38
Off the Payroll...39
Cry Baby 40
Independence..41
How a Man Saved the Universe....................................43
Kite Runner...44
Just a Note 45
The Wisdom of Master 46
O My Lord Which Turf Is Your Desire?.......................47
Hood of Individuality...48
Succumbing So Succumb 49
Mind of Man 50
Cosmos 51
Suck It Up! 52
Roar of the Lion 53
You Must Have Known This Better 54
Goose down Blanket Homage 55
Landing Birds 56
Secrets of Happiness 58
Math Is a Playful Power in Madness 59
WOW 60
Traps & Devices: In Search of Livelihood 62
Cry for Modern Man! Cry! 63

Dream of a Leaf 64
Heart Pumping Drill in Hot Pursuit 67
Dancing Flag Pole Avery Drummer 69
Vision: V-I-Si -On 70
Avoiding Entombment in Life 71
Welcome Back Home...72
Matter of Fact...73
In the Memory of Breeze..75
Room minus Rome...77
My Flag Will 78
Acculturation & Assimilation 79
Smell of Clean Oxygen 80
Contact Communication: Food and Entertainment .81
Eternity Revisited: 33 83
Be Ready 84
Structure of Structuration...85
Behave Yourself Then...86
Fingering the Revealed Secret: 2.................................87
Q: The Caesar's Scissor 88
Speechlessness...89
The Seventh English Curve 90
Man the Fragile..91
Vast Refugee Camp 92
Came Princess Camellia with Camel 93
Hindrance 94

About the Author 95

Introduction

After I was done with publication of the sixth volume of Star Light, **Stem & Leaf**, Trafford Publishing Company, 2011; I thought it was the last volume; wrapping up my entire poetic intellectual social emotional long journey in one and half thousand pages. There was no reason left for me to publish any more book of Stars Light poetry.

However, without much resistance, I found myself keep composing ever more poems, proses, and statements of which I was certain of their self-work contribution to artistic literary criticism. The composed work was piling up before my eyes looming ever larger, worthy, but I found no **raison d'etre** for their publication.

After passage of more than four years, one day out of boredom, I picked up a book of poetry I wrote myself for a casual reading in randomness. There, a poem I had written got my attention and it read as follow; the book was the fourth volume of Stars Light; **Sheida: Love Must Be Love**, Xlibris Publishing Company, 2008. Page 147.

The Posthumous

With due respect
I consider posthumous publications
As clear sing of Author's laziness
For once the author
Put his jeweled thoughts into the paper
He must fight with his tooth and nail
To get it out
Instead of hoping some unknown individuals
To pick up the chore in the future
That may or may not occur
I know... I know...
Given the conditions at the time
The chore is truly a real oppression to the core
But my friends
This is how the pyramid was built
Before Pharaoh getting ready
For his afterlife journey

Get up you lazy...!

From this unexpected "jolting" of poetry publication cardiac arrest, thus emerged this new volume of stars light into the being. It has been written and published against this poetic backdrop footprint that I left behind inadvertently during the course of my Socio-sociological journey. This effort was also augmented by the additional reasoning advantage that the previous posthumous publications were clearly lacking. No one else than the author himself knows better as to which poem to be eliminated and crossed, which one to be trimmed and edited in major way, and which ones to be embraced straight up as the major literary criticism deserving the spot light.

It goes without saying that this volume is the lion share of the piled up work that I have drilled through and "ran for it" for this collection and it's "*happily*" entitled: **Lights of the Dead**. This is divided in 2 different volumes so be sure to check **Volume 8**.

Whether or not there will be more jolting to trigger more "posthumous" work to appear by this author for a broader usage remains to be seen. In this regard, this author continues to remain hopeful since the light of stars is timelessly eternal, dead or alive, vis-à-vis, the short life span of man on earth in a comparative time sensitive perspective.

I must also say as a footnote for those who are familiar with both Farsi and English tongues that, I found a Farsi title for this volume in place of English one to be also quite appealing, perhaps either for its musical flow, parsimoniousness, or for its more of a respectful tone: **Anvare Dargozashtehgan.**

Turmoil Running Down Lava

Man does not need a sympathizer
To understand his pains
In sublime clean cut reciprocal communication in
listening
Instead....
He needs someone
To lift him up
To a higher ground
The land of love and tight embrace and kisses
Where down there
The running volcanic lava
Burning everything in its flowing downward river
path in hot steam!

ANCINET

The fire came out from the heart of earth
In roar and lightening in shake and burst
The thunder roar of fire was so loud
There was none who had not awaken from the rod
All stable rocks and mountains
Turned onto liquid fire rolling down to join the sea
There was no one who could see his loved one melting
down pouring down to sea
The fire was so loud...
No one could hear the loudest sound of man melting
down to sea
It was not the end of time
It was not the end of man
It was not the end of earth and mountains and rocks
But it was the rebirth of new world in roar and fire in
thunder and shake loud
Rolling down to see
To cool itself off in the sea
Like a molten iron
Until it turned into cold steel
Sharp strong self-aware in its rebirth and its repeal
The world was melting down
Rolling down to join the sea
In roar rumble, in fire, in shake, in lightening roar
vibration in burst
For the sake of man
For the survival of his ancient soul spirit

Food and Drink: Camelot
Revisiting the Infinity

My stomach is a sieve
No matter how much I drink
It is always empty looking for lease
It may be happy for few hours
But soon it is all upset going after all biting bees
My belly is riddled with many giant craters with giant holes
No matter how much softy or bulky food I am bringing in...
Soon it will become all empty asking to become quickly filled with a refill
The same is true for my lungs
Except every second
I need a quick refill
Or else I will become mad as hell and beyond the heal
This was only three elements of human needs on thy list
You have no idea how long the list will go on for this civilized beast
Now tell me are you ready to lead?

Should always remember that
His bird friends want to join him up in sky
But they just simply can't.
Being left alone
Comes with the territory
Not with abandonement.

The bird friends just left the action

Imagining Colors

I am pondering over the paradise flowers...
For they hardly yield to freeze & cold in their ever
blossoming resolve
Coming in infinite colors from which only a handful
of them exist in our world
Over one thousand primary colors
Where red and blue and yellow are only the secondary
derivative combinations...
Thanks for Magi residing inside the world imagine
Just to witness the birth of Christ in Bethlehem
Adoring him with their showering gifts
Thanks also for finding the "Nation" inside
"Imagination"
And a bright shining stable star born in the stable of
livestock
Instead of a terrifying and unstable lone angry comet
Only aiming to hit the earth in destruction

In paradise
How many secondary colors
One can derive from one thousand primary colors is
beyond description!
Impossible to comprehend and beyond wildest
imagination

In Praise of Laziness

Man who is working too hard
Will no longer be distinguishable from a machine
Like a fan working day and night
With no one paying any attention that it ever existed
let alone working
Rest!
So the noisy globe can get some rests too toward its
renewal
Good old times when winter was long and there was
nothing to do under fainted sun light
Enough of robotic country and robotic people

Flow of Life

The Bird was flying
Caterpillar was crying
The man was trying
A hiatus came in for a while in silence for eves
dropping
The lion went to his cool cave shelter for rest with his
cups still playing
The turtle calmly and slowly walking toward the river
The focused snake standing on its fragile feet tall
ready for striking,
The elephant pouring water on its head in shower to
cool off in hot summer that was drying,
The eagle kept looking with its radar eyes to zero in
on what is under water swimming carelessly
The deer jumped up and down in air to catch up with
the lover that was flying,
The tiger was tired ready for a nap, and
The sparrows kept making sex with no restrains or
cover with more babies hatching out quickly for flying
The baby lamb rushed innocently to reach her mother
nipple for sucking fresh milk in ecstasy---
The author kept editing the poems again and again see
if they are flying

Naked Earth, Naked Sky, Thunderbolts

Naked trees without leaves in winter
Are like the massive branched out bolts of lightning
in sky
Before the rain storm down pouring begins
Before the asserting thunder sound in rumble begins
It is so far away from us all
It takes months to hear their roar thunders in rain...
Or perhaps never
So far! Yet so close at reach in forest 'n in woods
Yes, the naked trees in bolts of lightning before your
eyes
Exist in a far way galaxy millions of light years away
from us
It is an optical illusion at its best!
Coming from a planet
Called: Planet Dream
It will save the man from extinction
Saving him from starvation
The tree lightning bolts coming from a planet dream

Lone Bird Star

A star bird star
That has flown way higher up in sky
Than the rest of bird flock
Should always remember that
His bird friends want to join him up in sky
But they just simply can't
Being left alone
Comes with the territory
Not with abandonment.

The bird friends just left the action

Bolts

There're days and there are days
There are hours and there are hours
There are minutes and there minutes
There are seconds and there and there bolts

Fresh Start

A leaf broke free from the tree in wind
With a touch down in dance with land
The sea wave swam in "SWELL" from afar 'n distance
All the way until reaching the shore line for a warm embrace

The ship left the coast line
But it will return with full hand to it once again
The student graduated from high school
But he will resume it at college again and higher up again
Child squanders his father's hard earned wealth without a sweat
Established families suddenly rootless traveling to unknown destinations
A happy family lay down the foundation of their brand new house
With infinite future & hope but it catches fire
Part of White House set on fire by the British on 1814
Now a landmark for show off to the welcomed guests
The car in freezing cold can't start despite the good battery put in place yesterday
A professional mountaineer die in avalanche for after 20 long minutes of struggle
An ambitious ski man breaks his both legs on the curve took for granted
A mother gives birth to a child inside a car on her way to hospital
And then star football player misses the easiest ball in universe before millions

Speedy train goes off the rail starts rolling on its roof
toward the destination
Passengers now are air born astronauts experiencing
weightlessness as glasses shatter
And the writes experience insomnia
Go behind the typewriters scribbling his red nose
"hoping"
It will come out as masterpiece to grant him a noble
peace prize
Since all have fallen in sleep

On a Grand Scale and on Large Scheme of Things

Sea is your dinner table!
Don't treat it as your toilet at the same time or any
other time
If not, then you will regret
What you have been eating so far

XXX

We have tendency
To lock the door behind
When we come and enter our home
To make sure it is one's shelter for rest free from harm
But the tragedy begins
When we forget to lock the
man-himself-the-shrine-the-house
From behind to protect it from the demon
That comes to steal his heart, mind, the soul, and
one's warmth and love, glory, and treasure
If you don't protect and lock yourself- the -house away
from the theft- the- demon who else?
Protect yourself from yourself by yourself
Put the lock and shackles on the intruders

DO NOT ENTER

In Search of Privacy

A man ran to the end of the world and
When reached his destination
Even before his sweat drying out
Someone greeted him by saying: Aligato, Ohio, Moshi
Moshi
We were waiting for you
W9hat took you so long
The member of our beloved family
The family of human kind.... Ohio!
The man in search of privacy said
I have just begun the journey
Come and run with me to the end of world
We got lots of leg work to do as well as mind
Aligato!

The work continuous....in search of privacy....

Social Oxygen

All my friends are gone
After having all those days of partying together
Now I am all by myself
Near this dream like pool...
Feeling lonely and bored...
I must head the city full of noise
To feel human again...
I feel suffocated with all the airs sucked out of my
lungs
As I sit next to this pristine large awesome pool on the
top hill
I am somewhat a bit nostalgic about their disorderly
conducts
Missing their mess...
It was planet good old earth...
Now it is planet Jupiter devoid of breathing air
Their floating cigarette butts and the trash in the pool
Was the blessing perhaps and was not so much a curse
So was the backed up toilet non-stop with no remorse
Now everything has come to a boring stand still

Nothing seems to move
Nothing!

Ocean Water Sand Clock

I was passing by a gentle sea in a cold morning
The clouds were hanging in suspension
Like a man suffering from a gloomy dark depressing
depression
An easy biological condition that can set man on the
path of anger and explosion
I am walking in the cold
Warming up bit by bit
As the biting cold on my skin becomes increasingly
more inconsequential
Now my mind is ready to pick things up for
inspiration....
Here I spot a small body of water on the sea shore
It looks like a sand clock but with sea water as
substitute in place of sands
The bottleneck of this clock was somewhat longer
than the standard sands
And the sea water entering to one box
Leaving out from the other end box back to sea again
Signaling the passage of measure timed by this sea
clock

Now the bottleneck is somewhat dry
And sea water has stopped entering running into the
sand clock box
Thus time has come to a stop....
But why?
Time has stopped
Since nothing of "importance" and "Significance" is
transpiring on earth
Propelling time toward life and flowing...

Time is the "Emperor" only flows and only flows for important things
Time cannot flow itself out
For meaningless things going into the oblivious absurdity
No extension!

Ocean! Is flowing, moving, cleansing relentlessly just like the time itself
Time is on Ocean side with pride with a long extension

Without Tomb Stone

I took an untimely nap today
Very untimely
Late later afternoon
An hour or so
I did not straighten up the bed cover very well
Like I always do like a good soldier during early phase
of training
Many wrinkles left in bend and bow on the cover
Here I am reading commenting on a book
Turn around by accident to look around for a bit break
time
Here I take a look at the wrinkled wavy bed up and
down
It looks like it is a cover over a dead person
No doubt it must be no one but myself
From head to toe gone under it the cover
Just the way I saw my dad when I found him gone
The bed cover was full of large flowers in design
Suggesting it is not a death bed with a blanket over
dead body
But a grave a resting place a tomb but with a new
design
Covered from head to toe with flowers
With no stone that one can speak of to seal off the
deal with carved out inscription

~~~~~~~~~~~~~~~~~~~~~
~~~~~~12~19~2014~~~~~~
~~~~~~~~~~~~~~~~~~~~~

The Country

Today, I wore my brand new gloves
It is modern, light, flexible, and warm up to some
temperature
But that morning was cold with deep sharp biting
teeth
These gloves gave me a chilling cold sensation
throughout my hands
As if they are made of sheets of ice
They triggered an old primordial dormant sensation
in my psyche in an awakening
When I was a first grader or so perhaps second
Walking in cold icy winter from home to the school
These gloves made me feel a second grader right there
and then back in time for real
With swollen engorged red hands punished by winter
cold
--Disciplinary act by the slashing beating freeze of
nature--
To get ready for the punishing education away from
the comfort of home
There I saw the flag installed on a tall straight pole
A large rectangular piece of fabric making sea waves
after waves in the wind
What they called "THE COUNTRY"

Here I am entering the warm classroom with hot
burning stove
At first I thought it was the kindest and loveliest
goddess
And it was
Trying to get to it as close as I could

With my nails feel like falling off my fingers in my red
swollen hands
At par with the burning red flame inside the stove in
coloration
Gradually started distancing myself from it bit by bit
Until I got out my jacket and wet boots off my body....
Listening more carefully to the teacher's instruction
by taking notes with warm fingers
There was time though when this stove goddess could
catch fire
Set itself ablaze for excess of oil dripping food into
its gut
Asking only for a hero to step inside
To throw this goddess burning stove right out of
classroom
Smashing crashing shattering window...
With bare hands with the loudest roaring vibration
loud in power with faith
To throw this proverbial bath water burning stove
right out into the school yard
Saving the school children inside--- "the country!"

Did I tell you about the tiny snapping lock that exists
in my modern glove?
Yes, when you take them off
You can use this tiny lock to hold the glove together in
pair
It looks like a glove handcuff when being put together
Admonishing you that enjoy your freedom without
going over the board
Until you hear a "mild" joyous hand clapping for you
For the fine things you have done for mankind

These gloves are way far better than Michael Jackson's
glittering auctioned off $200,000
For they have letter-number mixed password identity
When putting the lock on with its cute little snapping
sound

--------------------**18QS ><18QS**--------------------

"ONE"

In English language
The famous word, "money"
Was first born as "one"
To make sure
No one would or could claim it
As his own
Indeed, "my money" there is no such a word
Instead, o my god
O help me god

Cook the Messiah

It is my body!

O you cook
Don't tamper with food you are cooking
This is the body of king and body of the Christ, the
sage
You are preparing for man's survival
Including yourself as well
Do your job with honor and respect
As if you are making the best dish you can cook for
yourself
Before setting it up for your customers

Don't let the demon come poison your mind with his
plot
Save yourself!
Be an honorable cook at its best free from temptation

Be clean, sharp, and agile with hygiene
Even in the heat of summer
When you are before the blazing hellish burner in the
kitchen in sweat
With customers in line awaiting for your blessings

Original Sin Revisited

Man was born in the heaven
Then he was given the pairing gift of the woman
But, what is the "woman?"

Of course, the tangible universe, the Cosmo, and out
of the heaven
Thus, for man to complete himself
Man needs to listen to eve to the woman
To enter the real world, to gain the world, and out of
the heaven

Therefore
Behind every successful and "gracious" man in this all
out material world
There stands a woman

Repetition: To Have a Good Time

Time is a giant ocean wave
Man is the surfer
He must stand on the top of it in bend and bow
To have a good time while reaching the shore
If not
He dies under it with broken bones in suffocation
Of course there are high tide time
When the high wave of time collapses on itself in loud
rumble
To make a transparent tunnel for few short seconds
for the surfer
To ride the time right through without a hitch
And get lucky to "touch" the time itself for a second
with his own very hand
But he must watch out!
For tunnels are tunnels
Always run the risk of roof falling killing the miners
With the light at the end of time tunnel quickly
turning pitch dark with closing dead end
None of us are messiah
To walk on time with one step at a time calmly with
bare foot

As time has its high culminating points in constant
wave repetition
So should the man with his head above the water
Beware of time and its sharp biting tongue! Beware!
It is a mighty force to reckon with
Coming to get at you from unusual corners

Talk Obesity

Talking is like food
Once you started
You tend to go over the board
And then becomes habits over time
Keep on going over the board for ever more

See Fidel Castro with his talk obesity at old age
He hardly can utter a word these days
To enjoy his past time feast in festivity
When he was running marathon stand up behind the
dinner table podium
Eating speech-food with masses in ovation
Great man and woman are remembered
Only for few shiny words they uttered or wrote
somewhere

I know it is hard to exercise talk self-control
But you must start somewhere
In order to enjoy your old age retirement time
Still rocking with some appetite

Distinct Possibilities in Number

A leaf is targeted
Brought to Jet Propulsion Laboratory
All its characteristics are pin pointed in precision
And it is still intact in a tree
Season of autumn has arrived
One wonders
How many possible distinct snap shots
One can take from this falling flip flopping leaf
without repetition
Where...
Each snap shot is distinct from the other
Where…
All possibilities included and completely exhausted

A dive from high diving platform
Iterations begin and counted...counted! Counted!
It can't be infinite for sure!
It must be limited!
Muss es sein? Es muss sein!

I Am in Pain

I am in pain
But it is a different kind of pain
Not only there are no words available to describe them
But that I don't know myself what it is
It is a mystery pain
The only remote proxy description of it is
The feeling of endless convolution
While the air is sucked out of my lungs despite
breathing

The Moment, the Momentum, and the Momentous

Everything is a moment
In moment man finds wisdom new
In moment man loses his faith
In moment man falls in love and dies for its cause
In moment man is born
In moment somewhat in slow motion he dies
Not minute, not hours, but only a moment
Just like the heart beats
One beat in one moment at a time

Drink water without kissing it

If you don't break the time
Time will break you
What is time?
It is a stone that melts into air
It is air melting into stone
Bring lots of water into the time
To prevent it to become a stone
For if you don't water yourself who else
Drink water when the day about to leave to become
evening
It is in the twilight zone that time turns into stone
Though, you shouldn't be kissing the water!

Who knows?
Maybe man was first conceived as flower in the mind
of Lord
Yes, we just don't know...

My Claim: MC

From the things I have received from paradise
The laughter that I ever I got from hell
In the darkest moments of in life
I have to believe
With all evidence I have compiled
That…
God kept me glad
Sign that…
God loves me and few other things …
This and that also…
More than anything else in the universe

Beautiful snow falling….
When I made my claim on February 3, 2014
Hours not specified
Nor the minutes, neither the seconds

I bowed to sun, moon stars and clouds
I bowed to rive and sea and the oceans
I bowed to wind and fire
I bowed to trees in blossom and to earth soil
I bowed to many other things
I bowed…
I Bowed…
Now it is time to bow to myself & few other things

It Is All About the Lips! The Supreme!

To kiss something for the first time
You will be bonding to it
To have it ever more and more
Food, sex, love, child, etc.
Kiss nothing!
So you wouldn't have too much of something on your hands

Though when it comes to kissing
It is the easiest thing to say but the hardest thing to do
& follow

Trojan War

Food is a live spirit with biting teeth,
If you don't handle it right with the right rituals
To put yourself in the commanding position,
Once it got inside you,
It will kill you.
It is a lion that is coming in
Two strikes & out!

Anonymous

The most important things in life is
"To know"
There are people out there
Whether you know them or not
Who respects
Who supports
Appreciates
Cares
For who you are

Keep this in mind!
You are liked and loved by someone(s)!
The Anonymous!

Heart of Stones

After all running around in cold
To put chaotic things in order 'n in mold
With wind chill still blowing colder cold and more
cold
After all the work was done
I sat down exhausted fold inside fold and more folds
Yes I became conscience of myself without jolt in total
silence
Yes I have become cold stone untold in mold
Like a giant stone statue that you see sometimes in
winter cold
Except this giant has a beating heart inside this stone
untold

When I asked my who am I
I said then this must be the only heart of all stones

Silver and Gold: Christmas is a good time of the year

A man was made of pure gold with a pointing finger
Went before the mirror
That all of them are made of moon like silver without
exception
And said to the mirror
I know who you are
Your hands are open and know what cards you hold
You are a mixed bag and not pure at all and lesser of
value
You are not telling the truth
You are only part of the truth
The rest are lies

The silver man also pointed at the golden man
From the other side of world in separation and said
exact same thing

WEEW

Afar

Moon, tell me how much we love it...tell me
As it comes up with different make up and attire
different day and night
Sun, how much we adore it ...tell me
As it gently, hardly detectable, moving from the east
to the west unnoticeable
The stars, in bright clean cut pristine night, tell me
Forming constellations of various forms scattered as
neighbors in sky

But imagine one of the above for a short visit
Come down sits on our rest for a while

Now tell me!

Palm

You have no idea
How difficult it was to find the future
I traveled to far out stars
I visited colorful galaxy
Each with its own unique perfume
The Milky Way & I together had dinner on a round
table
Our conversation lasted nearly for eternity full of joy
I sat on the cotton clouds riding it to talk about love
with an all purple butterfly
I could easily jump and ride the butterfly
Yes that large and generous it was
Finally when a blue dew fell on my head
From that blue winking star with the smell of
pumpkin
I knew that it was time to go home with future now in
my palm
I got home
People were all busy with the present
So involved with the present
SO ENGULFED!

The future in my palm withered away
There was room for it in the engulfed present
It smelled like a fresh cotton cloud air dipped in honey
When it finally left my palm for good

Off the Payroll

The other day
I bumped into the angel of death dictionary in a
garage sale
It was a pocket book size and dusty and I bought it

When I got home I flipped through all pages
No matter how hard I tried...
The word "extension" was missing
I found the word "extraneous circumstances"
But no sign of the word "extension"
It was like a perfect set of teeth dictionary with a
missing toot

The second surprise in the angel of death dictionary
was that one page
Yes the entire one page, was set aside in constant
repetition for only one extended word:

Off the payroll
Off the payroll

Cry Baby

Companionship
Is like milk for a hungry baby...
I have seen the grown-ups and adults
Even with children and grand children
Literally crying for it milk out loud and without
shame
These are the few short moments in my life
That brings me laugh and more laughs

Independence

In the warm crystal clean river
The baby fish were hatched
The parents were all gone and can't be hacked

The baby fish formed a giant school fish for their own
protection
To make sure they could survive in river bed and last

The baby school fish now has gone much larger since
they were hashed
Now they venture out to the open sea to test their
caste
The giant school fish is a bit sluggish and not so fast

Now the seagulls join together to form a net to catch
this school fish in caste
The giant school fish can't escape from the seagulls'
circle in bombast
Each fish now is on its own since giant fish caught in
so fast
The seagulls now have the feast of their time
Catching one fish after another awesome and sublime

The net gets tighter and tighter until giant school fish
is all eaten and out of caste
Only few grown up baby fish can escape from the net
since they were hatched
Only those who learned to be independent

When they were the guest of giant fish school all in
latched
For they knew that
When they venture out to open sea
They must start off and be so quick 'n sharp 'n so fast
Until each becomes a giant fish without caste and
without bombast

How a Man Saved the Universe

Make you opinion,
Make sure your opinion is expressed and heard,
For it might be the only opinion
Among all the opinions in the universe
Worth listening to
That can help keep the earth on its right path
Rotating and moving....

Kite Runner

Moon
Stars
Sun
Are the kites up in Sky
Mankind is running on earth
To keep them up 'n high in sky
If man stops running
There will be nothing up in sky

The sky then would become utterly boring...
The kids find no reasons to look up into the sky

Just a Note

For sun light to reach man's eyes
It must go through infinite layers of filters
From the source to the destination
All the debris and pollutants and impurities particles
Are cleaned up during the journey
Just like a gross oil from the well
Until it becomes pure jet fuel for the flight

Therefore, be mindful when using man light
Particularly your computer screen with its asserting
big glare

Now let me go back to my remote village
Turn on my lantern to read some pages
Where there is no running water
No gas and no indoor plumbing and no and no
and no

The Wisdom of Master

A student went to an esteemed renowned teacher
Said, sir is there any word in this language
Of which you are its king …
You may not know its meaning?
The teacher replied in laughing said
Of course! There are so many words
In fact too many of them I don't not know what they
mean
So much so that if you pile them up on the top of each
other...
It will be such high mountain that no man has even
seen
Enough tall
After reaching its summit you & many touch the far
out stars with hands
The master was absolutely right on the mark!
Since the world of unknown will remain infinite
forever!

Then the teacher reminded all the students
The deadline for their new assignment due in next two
weeks

O My Lord Which Turf Is Your Desire?

When they are babies
They run sprinter in large group
In search of food
Barely flying
But when they're grown up
They're mostly flying
Hardly walking let alone running
In their search of livelihood

From these sea birds
One can say
The air belongs to the grown ups
And the land to the growing ups
As long as each
Remains active in their own turf & domain

What kind of birds they are
What their name is
This time it is top secret!
Their identity cannot be revealed!

Hood of Individuality

A child is born
Suddenly....
A large number of people
Get a new title along all the other titles that they
have had
The child deep in sleep in her crib motionless doing
nothing
Yet the ripple effect of title-hood keeps on rolling
multiplying expanding
In the calm lake of human relations and
connected-hood-ness

Soon the child will stand up on her own feet in her
proverbial crib
In this stormy and not so calm world
To search for her own title
To mark her own title
By her own and for her own and by her own
To leave her foot print of title-hood-ness on this world
Unique onto itself like her own very unique foot print
That is now in her mouth in sleep
Sucking it dry
As the substitute and improvisation already for her
mom's missing nipples dull of milk
That should have no ripple effect at all
But straight down to the throat and down to the
tommy

Succumbing So Succumb

Some hours are longer than usual...
This is the nature of time...
Its units whatever they are
Are not only made of extremities
But also of extreme flexibility...
Some hours stretch so much and so far that
They become months if not years...and vice versus

And it is in this brutal flexibility of time that
No matter how hard the man tries his best
To drill his way through this tunnel
For arriving at the next hour
Prove futile and impossible

He never manages to get out of the tunnel
He succumbs to the tunnel

Stark and no stark trees
Now drilling through the tunnel in cold winter
With the hope of seeing the first day of spring
The living dead is drilling through

Mind of Man

Mind of man
Is like a fire pit
Sometimes is dead cold
And nothing can turn it on
Sometimes it is hot and kicking
Nothing can turn it down or off

If man learns to keep both extremities in check and
balance
He surely will have something to eat 'n good
When his supper time comes up
And that one won't be his last one

Man is the creature of extreme and extremity!

Cosmos

Man by nature
Wants diversity, not monotony;
Different foods,
Different friends,
Different places,
Different loves...
Different...
Different cars...
Different neighborhoods,
Different...

Which country,
Thus far,
In the world,
Has fulfilled
This very basic primordial human desire at its very
best?

Suck It Up!

Do your share
Do your work
Do your best of your bests
It will eventually echo hard enough
So hard that that who must hear it
In order to prompt into action on your good behalf
He will be hearing it

The world is inter-connected!
Action begets reaction in the large scheme of things
It is a promise of galaxy looming at large

Roar of the Lion

There are death moments in life
In wickedly stand still
Nothing moves
Even your lungs during the breathing
All corridors are shut tight
Like a prison cell with inmate in awaiting for
execution

A glass of sublime wine
After the color of man's blood
Surely is sure revolution!
Towards man's joy in ecstasy

Now as wind blows in motion
To shake trees
To sing their songs
Before the assembled leaves musicians

The frozen river begins to follow …

You Must Have Known This Better

An all-out accomplished person
Who constantly puts behind
A trail of obvious failures and mistakes
That can be easily detected and listed
By any ordinary and not so accomplished common
person,
Can easily ruin all the accomplished person's
accomplishments and achievements
Into dust and powder in the wind and the subject of
ridicules---
Worst, it can hurt their income in a very
substantial way
All the way to turn them into a destitute accomplished
man dying in poverty...
Alone and abandoned in cold.

All are on the record

Goose down Blanket Homage

Each snow flake is a bright star
There are infinite number of them
All coming down in dance, bow, and gratitude
To pay homage to earth
For providing livelihood to Adam & Eve
After they put their hard work in sweat on thy land

The farm land is carpeted with peace in quiet silence
after dance
The farm land is offered a warm white blanket for a
long winter rest
It is all fluffy-thick- light-weight –warm- goose-down-
feather-blanket with no lance
Until spring when it rises in bounce and in pounce
and back
For its own stems upwardly mobile for harvest with
slow romantic dance
After that wintery long good night sleep with lots of
rest under goose down in lance

Landing Birds

The bird leaves
Now all are fully well grown and quite heavy weight
Somewhat angry, bitter, unhappy, resentful, and
depressed
Experiencing impoverishing self-esteem
With diminishing responsibilities & increased
idleness
They must be weaned out and separated from their
feeding mother
To leave their lofty positions
Before the exit
The inevitable departure
They must change color
Wear their new dress uniform battle
The color of flight in descent
Their new dress worn sign of detachment from the
mother
With no point of return

They are now flocking in great numbers
To land in search of food
This time it will not be so easy
Instead
It will be a hard harsh crushing fight and heart
wrenching battle
In carving out one's livelihood
Worse they are now in the company of so many
strangers
Hardly ever known to them before separation
When they were on their soft parent's laps taking sun
bath up there

In search of food and affection and love
Leaves birds must descend
From high altitude to low destitute
There is no alternative...
And from there on
They will become permanent homeless drifters with
no power at their disposal
Drifting to here and there like poor mentally ill
chronic alcoholics
At the whim of wind at play of its own desire

These once happy singing charming cheerful proud
sweet playful lofty birds
Every day now gets smaller and more broken apart
and more humiliated
Until they become food to be spoon fed to the
devouring land itself with crushing gravity

There is no alternative....

Secrets of Happiness

Besides all the great teachers of happiness in the world
There are two special ones
Surpass them all and
They both are so close to you
You are not even aware of them most of the time

One is heart
The other lungs
In constant locomotion
Motion,
Movement
Ebbs and flow
Guaranteeing the happiness unhindered

Follow these two great teachers all the way to your last
minutes of life...
The most forgetful and most difficult following!

Math Is a Playful Power in Madness

My birth year
Is a mathematical wonder
Simultaneously wonderful in two separate worlds

1952 A.D. = 61*2^5

1331 A.H. = 11^3

621 Standard Gap = 69*3^2

2001 (Attention: Beware of Dog) = 69*29

Each is a can of worms meant to be opened up for
more wonders

I share this noble math on a condition
Not to ask further about the birth month and
birth day
For each separate world
For it will be too wonderful of meta-mathematics
Too complicated for anyone to handle its cosmological
significance
Enjoy its wonders for now
And don't indulge in this case or in any other case in
the future
For over-indulgence is the cause of many ailments

Okay my body friend body?

WOW

Some people are like a house
After some long years you go visit them
You see their lush green flowery gardens are all gone
In their place long weeds with seeds ready and all
done
The solid roof in great color has vanished
Instead the leaking one with big hole put in and the
banished
The pretty sun room that we used to drink and chat
and play with cat on the side
Is now crumbled burned to the ground

The kitchen that we used to keep it clean and shiny
With delicious food for friends and family on table in
the oven getting ready
Now is now smothered 'n gone
In its place"
On a mission, rats and filthy cock roaches in there just
keep on running

The living room where the food was served and the
radio listened
It has also tarnished
Instead the four legs dining table has become two
legs one
Like a sinking ship in a stormy sea destined to be
perished
Most pretty rugs and carpets are now spooky and
rotten
With ugly liquid jelly like stain spreading as its new
polish

Those pretty windows that used to be clean and
transparent
From where we used to see the dance of falling snow
now all disappeared
Instead the broken messy glasses with sharp edge
bleeding
With the song of distant bird heard pleading and
crying

Now most of the steps in the stair case are missing
Like an old man with no teeth in his mouth laughing
in anger

The beds we used to sleep and rest in perfume
dreaming
Now is ripped open with yellowish cottons spreading
A Nesting place for lice for an unhindered procreation

The shiny bath tub that we used to wash our bodies
In cold winter in hot water warmth
With Soap opera foams followed
Now has fallen from the second floor to the basement
With no hot shower and itself submerged in dirty
dark leaking pothole of oil

I will revisit myself ten years from now
See If I am living in that house with a sorrow sound of
"WOW"

Traps & Devices: In Search of Livelihood

The architectures of ideology
Deliberately put inside their structure
Deliberate and obvious errors and acts of mistakes
Enough obvious
That any novice can identify them for criticism
This is where the snare trap device comes into work
To catch the victims for food and otherwise life necessity
By boosting the victim pride
With their own well construed erroneous nonsenses

Cry for Modern Man! Cry!

Modern man as he walks farther
On the path of modernity and complex civilization
The list of needs also gets longer and more diverse
All the while population multiply exponentially

Every time, you mention an item
Might be eliminated from his long list of needs
Due to exhaustion of natural resources,
He raises his both hands over his head in surrender
To have it back ASAP!
Surrender!
Item number on the needs list; 100,000th: Hot shower

The little tiny birdy with his little thin feather coat fur
Singing song in the midst of stormy winter bur bur
I will ride out this cloud with this same set of clothing
for sure
Until the spring comes to show off this same dress
In glamour on run way fashion on zeal for more tour
In blossom in perfume and love with music and with
soft roar
The little birdy is anorexic eating only few seeds and
few more corn seeds
And trust no builders
To fix his shelter high up when feeding his baby with
some soft meals

Dream of a Leaf

A leaf is born
Enjoying the sun light for the first time
The breeze of spring on its baby fresh skin as well
Immediately it gets back to work
To process the gross into the pure juice
From where fruits and tree itself grows
It is a multi-task creature doing all at once in
perfection
Breathing oxygen into the world
Making shelter for mankind from woods I sweat to
make
The fire to warm up his house and to cook his food
To create layers of dark rich precious top soil that
greedy world is scooping it up with no shame
Making music in breeze for mankind awaiting for its
heavenly song
And even when man & woman were in residence in
paradise
Helping them cover themselves in grace in thin layer
of magnificent silk leaf
Performs miracles after miracle this ultrathin creature
One of which making the invisible in sky visible
That no one could have imagined it seeing it before
Yes, the invisible air made visible
With the dancing and singing of leaves in wind with
tangible hard evidence for documentation
Another, pulling out messianic new color from its
sleeves in fall that never seen before
Turning water to wine from green to red to yellow,
brown, purple, white

Yes, when in fall it falls on water it walks on water for quite long distance
With the help of his long time invisible friend, wind in waves
Turning itself into a writing pages for the ancient sages to keep their script more endurable and safe
On and on and on ...and the list goes on...
Sometimes, other arduous tasks performed by its sword like sharp body
Not recognized at all by the world for lack of its sensitivities & sensibilities
Has anyone in the world flipped a leaf over to see its back?
To see it is filled with branches of blood veins swelled up with life pressure
Not so visible on its typical surface face value
Leaf hides its tormented vein vessels in pain from the world unlike the hand of man
The list goes on! But what is the dream of leaf so busy at work?
While the beating continues
On its fragile body leaving holes after holes of suffering mark like Swiss cheese
Or like star constellations in "leaf sky" at night for man to find his way lost at sea
Yes, to become a bird
Crossing its finger when its flight time departure begins and arrives
The wind will be strong enough
To take this bird into a farther and farther distance ever dreamt of
All the work and suffering done only for one "moment"

The moment of transformation to become a flying bird...free
With its stem tail helping it to navigate right in an uncharted terrain
Where no leaf has ever gone before... the final frontier...the leaf star space enterprise

Heart Pumping Drill in Hot Pursuit

Heart is a pump
Imagined it is armed with a sharp point for drilling
That is heart is heart a pumping drill
Constantly in combustion
Expansion and contraction
To make the drill work in penetrating penetrated
penetration
The journey is long
At the end is where the goal sits
And all the drilling done toward reaching this goal

In this relentless penetration
Several million light years of distance must be drilled
through
And sometimes there are sad cases of breakdown
The pump malfunctions
The drill itself breaks down inside the tunnel shaft
Or some unusual objects found in the drill journey
simply impenetrable

Now the question is
What is "it" that this heart pumping drill is after "IT"
in hot pursuit?
With beating that seems never plan to stop until to
get "IT"

Even in exceptional case of monarch death
Pharaoh allows all his organs to be removed before
burial
But his pumping heart drill kept inside his chest still
intact

So he can begin drilling again during his new life after this life after life

Therefore, hold on tight to this heart
You need it badly
In this world and in the other world, and in this life and in after life

Tool! It is yours! You own it! You keep it! You take care of it!
One thing closer to you than your wallet
Search for it nowhere else but inside your chest

Dancing Flag Pole Avery Drummer

The wind was heavy and blowing
The temperature was plummeting too low in crying
The freezing wind chilled cold was fast and faster and
flying
The sea in the background still keep making roaring
waves tall in climbing
There was a steel flag pole without a flag
Tall ...standing, shivering and trying
A bit loose on the top and in the middle in cold and
thus shake still trying
It became a drummer for all the heavy wind blowing
The music came from the flag pole now as drummer
in drumming
Unheard of or played out by any of the known
drummer when hit hot in flying
The speed and Rhythm of beatings was so
phenomenal
Could not be copy catted by any renowned world class
drummer even if he crying
A man near death from this cold or even in his grave
Could not resist not dancing to this flag pole in
drumming
There was only one drum and one drummer and one
wind
But in this cold
Thousands of masterly written music notes
Were played in second effortlessly and with no trying

Vision: V-I-Si -On

I draw them a picture
Asked them
What it is that?
They uniformly pointed to some common ground of
what that picture is
Then I wrote a poem about the picture
They began to see a new picture
I wrote another one
They too began see one new one
The third, the fourth, the fifth, the sixth, the seventh
ones were written
So does the new way of new ways of seeing the same
picture

Conclusion?
Man by nature is socially blind
He can't see a thing
He needs to be guided by a visionary
To help him see
The things that he needs to see
From time to time different take and different
interpretation
As life shifts, emerges, changes
From same identical picture of life itself

We only cross our fingers for those who give us vision
To be the right ones
Not the fools and not the lunatics
What is it that I see?
Just suck it up! To the best of your ability
Until the light can be seen at the end of tunnel

Avoiding Entombment in Life

Get out of itself
From itself
By itself
For itself

Now
You
Have
Self

Earth itself
Goes through
Earthquake, shake, and rumbles
Doing its best
To get out of its own entombment self
Like giant whales
Leaving the sea flying for air
Plunging back to the sea in massive splash
Getting rid of all the built up layers of parasites
entombment

Defying gravity!

Welcome Back Home

After a long hard journey in hardship
Leaving their country and their country man behind
Arriving in the new land
In so many unbelievable ways and routes seems nearly
impossible
Bringing their properties and wealth piece by piece
Like small ants carrying stuff in their mouth in long
line
And eventually become the citizen of the new land
You see them again despite their oath of departure
and arrival
Conglomerate, congregate, and concentrate in their
own ethnic enclaves
Little Tokyo, Little Korea, little Tehran, little Kabul,
little of this and little of that
As if during oath citizenship ceremony
They were taking the oath to go back home this time
fresh
And to live in peace and harmony
With their own kind exclusively and only
With doors shut tight to foreigners and outsiders
What does man really want from this world?
One thing though is for sure
We cannot relocate from earth to somewhere else
And we cannot get away from our own kind
No matter how difficult of a journey path route one
has taken

Matter of Fact

It doesn't matter what happens to me
What matters is what happens to you
That is after what happens to me
Yes! It does matter to you!
Why? Because it is all matters and all bodies and all
materials
Whether subjectively or objectively
Do you hear?
I don't care what happens to me
But you must care about what happens to me
For what happens to me
Will be magnified in force and then shoved many
times and then will happen to you
Matter of fact is: matter is face of life
One of which is being wedded is a good thing
For if one matter is not working out well for you
You can move from that matter to the next matter
After separation from the first one and even the
second one
But don't forget!
Matter does matter!
That's why wedding is a high matter
And should be treated that way
When wedding time comes for celebration
With the prospect of possible divorce
When it becomes rude & inconsiderate like wild dog
infected with rabies
Despite its relatively high majestic level devoid of
demeaning label
And there are matters and then there are matters
Of course man by nature is always after the better one

That is why everyone's wish is to become a king
For it is the mother or father of all matters
The best and the highest

The majestic matter!

In the Memory of Breeze

Don't get me wrong
I believe in freedom
In fact this is the most precious jewel
That man should be holding on to
Taking any measure necessary to preserve it
Including the things under more dire circumstances
He shouldn't do!

But hay be realistic
The Stone-Age gene is still within us
When there was nothing out there but "cruel" Mother
Nature
What is the point?
Well, once in a while travel to your primordial Stone-
Age life memory
To be in a world where there is no technology
Yes, you are in a prison cell
With prison bar window open only in an empty room
Helping you to work out
As breeze blows gently into your self-imposed prison
cell

Can you go to your room alone for heaven sake
spending few hours?
Without jittering and agitation
To look upon yourself to know what you want
Be fire this prison cell

After all you are a prison onto yourself with skin all around you in shackle
With the autumn breeze coming in
To help sort things out with clarity that your mind desires
See Michael Jackson tried to get out of his skin prison cell prematurely
Despite all the moon dance he did in weightlessness on his slippery cute shoes
With never getting the chance of winning the golden mask before the burial
Yes, nothing comes easy
You need "to do time" inside your skin prison cell with no easy way out!

Room minus Rome

It is
That excess of
That thing
That will lead man
Into the blindness
With eyes shut wide open--

More Room minus Rome!

My Flag Will

The poems I wrote
All are penned in plain black
And printed on plain white paper
Dip each word not letter in color and in more colors
You will see suddenly
The sale will multiply exponentially
Even the psychedelic fools and not so fools
Will find a way to string the words of the same color
together
From where
A new-bizarre-beyond-this-world poetry book could
emerge with meanings
Showering the world
With poetic colors coming from the unknown world,
unknown source and unknown horizon
I assure you from this randomness of colors in
existing written meanings
The new meanings in metaphor, analogy and
combination imagination
Will spring up to life
As if one having a joyous poetic journey high on LSD
Transcending this boring mundane reality to a higher
uncharted trip

Small colorful pocket poetry book to be read to get
out of this!
While sitting in a crowded subway train heading the
boring all rational work place

Acculturation & Assimilation

Society is like a running molten lava in running
The moment you step in
You become part of it
With all idiosyncratic uniqueness vanished

The "struggle" then is
Keeping your soul in this sociological inferno
Preserved just like the red rose in perfume
In a cool early morning with dew as its honored
welcomed guest

Yes! Apocalypse!

Smell of Clean Oxygen

As I was kissing her tight lip to lip
With nose pressed nearly hard on the cheek
I realized in split second in light and thunder "that"
This is what breathing pure oxygen really meant to be
I breathed more and more
Through her skin cheek oxygen purification purifier

Tomorrow I will put on my running shoes
Dash in a flash to the congress quarter
To put my petition in an expeditious motion on the
floor
Which is
To put clean air act proposal into the law
With tooth and nail hammered in bold and mighty
Stronger than the dinosaur's

Contact Communication: Food and Entertainment

The Seagull was flying
It was a windy day
So the seagull was effortlessly flying without trying
Like a hummingbird frozen in the air ready for gliding
I began to whistle so the air born seagull in stand still could hear my trying
For I notice and knew that
Seagull was enormously enjoying her effortless stand still in flying
I was right!
The seagull responded to my whistle by keeping hummingbird type flying
I kept on whistling and the seagull kept flying on and on and on without trying
My whistling worked as tight thread holding the seagulls kite firm in air happy and no drying

Until her friends came join this seagull to get her for real time in flying
I knew what his friends told that seagull in air but without flying

If you keep staying in air and in freeze without trying
And keep listening to Hassan's whistling

Enjoying his applause and recognition of you without
trying
You will starve to death with this wind with no effort
and no trying
Come join us in search of food
With wind or without it but keep on with effort and
only trying

Eternity Revisited: 33

The universe of unknown
Is truly infinite
Always opportunity for man
Convert a good chunk of it
Into the known
Into the more or less tangible knowledge.

Don't worry
It is not like our planet nature resources
Finite and exhaustible
It is out there for man to explore and to find out more
Finally we got a good news in this gloomy world:
It will never ever run out!
And there is always left something to do

Be Ready

People of fame
Are different than the ordinary one—
You think you know them when you see them on the
stage
But when you get close to them,
Person to person
Be ready to find another person to your utter
surprise—
For "it" is not what you think it is!

A little tired...
Very little nerve left for playful play these days

Structure of Structuration

Everyone talks about foundation
Foundation... the founders...
Yet one wishes to get the heck out of the foundation
Instead go up ever faster
Toward a more upwardly mobile world
Out of the foundation...

Since there is a total black out in the foundation
Totally vacant and empty in vacuum
Then all of sudden
A shadowy group
No one knew who they are
Just a year ago,
Emerge and terrorize
The upwardly mobile societies around the globe with
no base
Causing the entire the civilized and not so-civilized
world
To get united as one unified front to fight this
"spontaneous creation"
With Pastor's germ free preservation pasteurization
Do you know the name of "IT"
I am referring to
In my constant nonsensical incoherent ramblings?

Behave Yourself Then

When people ask you questions
About your actions
Behaviors...
The master answer
To any question and all questions is only one:

I Am "a" Citizen!

If pressed too hard
Then add
What you do for living

Fingering the Revealed Secret: 2

Sign of great work of art
*I*s only one
No matter how voluminous
You eat from it
You never feel too full
Always more room left for more
Nearly at par with fresh air one breathes

Q: The Caesar's Scissor

Worry beads
Vulnerable to scissor
Toward its disintegration in disarray
When internal hidden thread
Exposed during the play
When beads coming in
One after another with no end in sight—
The Caesar Emperor may rip it apart
With his scissor
If not used in its proper time and place:
The praying time and meditation
As the exposed thread
Has spiritual immunity from the harm

Speechlessness

From
All
The
Jaw dropping
Innovations
Man
Has
Come up with
None quite matches
The magic of
Bicycle

The Seventh English Curve

Live:

Life
Without
Love
Is not only a lie
But also
An evil vile
As well.
Friends…
Levi
Is hungry

Man the Fragile

Avoid
Compromising
Situation
For this is where the man's strongest will
Melts away into the oblivion
Yes, this is how weak a strong willed man is--

Get Covered!

Vast Refugee Camp

Man in misery
Easily settles
For less and lesser and the least
His prides
Dangerously
Bitterly vanishes....
As he falls from the top
To bottom of the pyramid hierarchy of needs

In the midst of it all
There comes
Miraculous exceptions
In awe
To prove
Man is man after all
Who build pyramid
In the first place

Came Princess Camellia with Camel

In Middle Eastern culture
Revengeful Camel
Known to hold on to bad memory
For an extremely very long period of time
For its past mistreatment
More than any other species

There …
After reaching the destination
It is time to keep the camel outside
With his undesirable character
Instead let the most sublime human characters
Go on, persist, and shine on:
Forget, forgive and happiness and celebration
Do you know what I am speaking of?

Ride the camel and don't let the camel ride you
For you may need the camel to cross the barren desert
again
Where human needs stand at its most bare minimal
expectations

Hindrance

The artist
Inside the burning fire hell singing
The musicians too improvising inside this torture
chamber
Gradually all are set ablaze on fire at par with the hell
itself rising
The explosion is becoming more explosive as time
goes by deeper
Every ounce of energy is sacrificed in the union with
the inferno
Still with all these hellish improvisations
The artist is not hot enough
To carry his message loud and clear
To "THAT"
Who is standing tall above and beyond the rising fire
hell fire
Possessing the loud
Except in rare cases
Even breaking the guitars
Crying
Pleading
Shouting
Crashing the microphones hitting against the wall
Jumping off the stage in rampage
Flip flopping in the cage
Is never loud enough to be heard without hindrance
There is nothing to be done
But keep on burning inside the fire
Never good enough
To please the one to be pleased
Louder!

About the Author

Abol Danesh, the fourth child, grew up with his four siblings of two brothers and two sisters in a well educated family environment with modern values.

All the way to fifth grade, Abol Danesh was the only boy in an all girl elementary school. Abol Danesh's mother, the principal of school, made the exception to all girls school protocol for her youngest son. She was running one of the most successful and upbeat elementary schools in town and believed that she deserves that exception in order to give a firm foundation education to her own son who was honored right at birth to have his father's name exclusively among his two other brothers, Abol!

After graduation from an elite high school in mathematics, he went on to study Accounting and Management in the prestigious Tehran University. From every thousand participants in the entry exam only very few could be admitted after passing tough admission exams with high marks.

After graduation, Abol Danesh, by passed the remaining of compulsory military service by pursuing higher education abroad. That was the provisional exception authorized by the Emperor of Persia along with the approval of cultural council for those who were eager to pursue higher education abroad. Abol Danesh, chose the field of Sociology, despite the demanding requirement of the advanced mastery of Complex and highly sophisticated Sociological

English language. In the face of prevailing obstacles, however, Abol Danesh earned the master degree from California State University at Los Angeles in Sociology while a year earlier embarked on a Ph.D. program in the prestigious University of California, Riverside. In 1985, he was awarded the Doctoral of Philosophy in Sociology. He broke three type writers while using them day and night to finish up his dissertation in a windowless office due to "Do or Die" time limitation.

With doctoral degree at hand, Abol Danesh Landed a visiting assistant professorship position at Colby College. An ivory tower four year liberal art college that particularly catered to the pool of well off well versed and highly advanced educated students with strong background, many of whom had already finished major literature literary work such as Shakespeare before their puberty age. His one year term contract year after year was extended at the end of each year for four years with distinction while two of his daughters were born in the State of Maine.

From there on, Abol Danesh ventured for a permanent professorship in sociology. After four years of teaching, service, and research at the University of Rhode Island, he was awarded tenure professorship. Permanent!

Abol Danesh, published the dissertation and several books and articles in his field of development, inequality, and urbanization. Whether it was accident or plan of life, Abol Danesh suddenly began to show interest in poetry and poetry writing but in pure isolation, the same way earlier he shifted the course of his work and attention away from accounting to sociology, where he could finish up his CPA in accounting in less than three years. According to Abol Danesh, this new course of work should be understood as "Socopoetry;" an uncharted marriage of sociology and poetry in an unusual way filled with creative explosions and sudden bewilderment in dream like sociological roller coaster awakening.

The author published six volumes of poetry, or Socopoetry if to use his own coined term, under the rubric of Stars Light in over one and half thousand pages in span of ten years. The dominant themes of these poems are hopes as blue print toward resurrection from the dead and rejuvenation away from decay and atrophy; a dream like permanent pipe lining between the creative literature and the standing pyramids

Two additional surprising volumes, follow up of Stars Light, now before the eyes of esteemed readers, "Lights of the Dead" should be considered as books that should have been published posthumously but for the reasons expounded in the introduction, these books are out for public usage all because of the sheer luck! For Abol Danesh, is truly a fortunate man who could crawl out of the grave, finish up the dirty dishes and publish the work that were scattered all over in disarray in mess.

Abol Danesh has lived for an extended period of time in Maine, Rhode Island, and California for educational academic purposes.

If one adds the author's first inititial to the aforementioned states' abbreviations in the United States, one could arrive "in" "AMERICA." Of course, such things are exceptions and don't happen often, thus, they should be considered as Good Fortune Omen Socopoetry: GFOS

Abol Danesh not only has been enjoying biking, gardening, running, and long distance walking in the heat of which he is cooking his voluminous "Socopoetry", but also mountain climbing as well. Abol Danesh for several times reached the summit of Mt. Whitney in America and once Mt. Tochal in Persia, both about 14,000 feet elevation above the sea level.

Abol Danesh, since his late twenty, has become a bit hard on hearing because of practice shooting, during his stay in California. There was no one in the wild wide wilderness to tell him so to cover his ears when pulling the trigger of his loud Remington rifle and the double barrel shot gun filled with heavy duty bear killing buck shells.

Abol Danesh has been diagnosed with unclassified "Depression Disorder" illness with code number 311 for quite many years. He has been continuously blue since 1999.

Printed in the United States
By Bookmasters